PEOPLE PROBLEMS
&
NEGOTIATION

People Problems & Negotiation
Author Philip K Sinclair (Phil)
t/a Leader's-Edge RSA

Published by Leader's-Edge 2012
Copyright Phil Sinclair

The entire copyright of this publication including all intellectual rights are the property of the publisher. The book is sold subject to the condition that it shall not in full, or in part, by way of trade, or otherwise, be resold, hired out, copied or stored in an electronic retrieval system other than that of the purchaser, or circulated in any form without the publisher's consent.

CONTENTS

Part One- People Problems
Introduction
Leadership Communication
Eight Foundations
Techniques
Dealing with Anger
Behaviour Modelling
Conflict Resolution
Summary

Part Two- Negotiation
Introduction
Conflict & Mutual Interest Bargaining
Pre-negotiation, Research & Planning
Prepare for Active Listening
The Presentation Process
The Bargaining Process
Picking up Concessions
Reaching Agreement
Negotiation Tactics
Summary

INTRODUCTION

If everybody were to follow you unquestionably as their leader and totally embrace the mission statement of your business, life would be just great. And you wouldn't be needing this book.
But you get people who just aren't motivated about you as their manager or about the job they do for a living. Some of them are even actively negative causing disruption and sometimes destruction of what you are trying to achieve. Then there are those who might just have some problem holding them back from being otherwise productive, useful and motivated members of your team.

Part One of this book will help you to understand these situations and how to handle them and the effects that they have on you personally and on your business as a whole, by using a process of "Open Communication".

Part Two of this book is also People Management of a kind. It will teach you that nearly everything that you want to acquire or achieve comes through a process of negotiation. Everything is negotiable. But how do you do it so that you achieve your objectives in such a way that the other party doesn't feel hard-done-by. Or should you care how they feel as long as you win? This book outlines the principles of major negotiation and provides you with the tools to make it a valuable lifelong skill that gives you what I call "The Leader's-Edge". Principles of large and very important sit-down negotiations are the same as may be used in part, or whole, in your everyday life whatever it is you want to "buy" or "sell". Consider this; if you don't know how to effectively negotiate, there are others who do – and they will expect to win when they meet you.

PART ONE
PEOPLE PROBLEMS

Dealing with people and people problems on a one-to-one basis is really a matter of using the skill of "Open Communication". When you have this skill you will be able effectively to deal with a variety of situations from anger to conflict, to poor performance. You will be able to use systematically good communications techniques to modify behaviour in others so as to produce better performance, better rapport and more willingness to accept and work with you as team leader.

I hope this book will make you think more constructively and purposefully about People and Problem Management. It will make you question your assumptions and even shift your entire thinking about communication into another, more versatile, gear. When you realise that communication is a circle which is only successfully complete when absolute understanding has taken place between the transmitter of the message and the receiver of the message, much rests on you, the leader, to make the communication successful.

It means that you need to recognise a great deal about where the other person is coming from, emotionally as well as their habits and <u>their</u> preferred style of communication, their goals, their objectives and their comfort zones. It means that you need to understand their behaviour and have the tools to explore behind the behaviour to reveal what is prompting it. It means that you must know how to explain what behaviour you want and to replace the behaviour that you might find unacceptable, in such a way that it becomes all quite <u>acceptable</u> to the other person. None of this is an easy task. But then neither is taking up the challenge of leadership!

- Open-communication has to be a two-way street and so we're going to start today on

<u>your</u> side of the road ahead. That is the leader's side! We'll begin by discussing the eight foundations of leadership communication, all of which help you to become open in your communication.

Open communication is recognised by managers and leaders today as the right way to communicate, if you want to cultivate a team of motivated followers who willingly turn on extra steam for you.

Communication is more than talking!

Telling someone to do something isn't necessarily communicating what it is you want done. Communicating might involve you <u>showing</u> them what it is you want done...or demonstrating how to do something. It will certainly involve body language and it must definitely involve <u>active listening.</u> Communication is also as much an emotional transmission as a practical physical message. You, as a leader, are expected to lead the communication process when dealing one-on-one with your peers and your subordinates. So let's run through the eight foundations of leadership communication.

1. Look for good intentions in a relationship - rather than a quick fix of a problem

Leader's look for <u>ongoing</u> relationships and therefore use communications skills to explore and develop relationship opportunities. Each time that they meet with the same person, or team of people, they will look for ways of increasing their understanding and co-operation with that person, or those people. Of course finding a solution to the problems that these people bring you is very important but after the problem is removed there is still the person. . .and if you have helped a person to get through a problem the chances are they will respect you more and want to follow you. As a leader you must have good intentions. There cannot be free and open communication if you have secret agendas, or schemes, up your sleeve that might leave the other person with a worse problem than before they spoke to you. Also, try never to break a communication ...if things get really hot, argumentative and full of conflict, you can always walk away and pick up the communication again at another time. Leader's don't <u>burn</u> communication bridges... rather they are always trying to <u>build</u> communications bridges.

2. Be prepared to use authority and NOT authoritarianism!

Leaders are successful people with power over other people. Wherever possible you must resist using your power in an authoritarian way. Authoritarianism forces people to do things that they may not necessarily want to do, with the result that those people feel reluctance and withdraw their support. They close up and communicate only as little as possible. You can display that you have authority without making people fearful of you.

When people are respectful about the way you captain their ship for them they become naturally accepting of your authority and your leadership...and they become more open in their communication of a free flow of solutions and ideas. You and they must both practise open-communication in order to inspire responsible and creative thinking

3. Learning to break old habits...is the third foundation of good open-communication .

Maybe you've spent a lifetime of giving out orders and instructions on how to do things... in which case you might easily have fallen into the habit of doing the same things in the same way every time that those things come up.

Maybe your way works for you...but does it work well for the other person? Is the communication circle really complete? Do you always use the same body language? Are you even <u>aware</u> of your body language? Do you generally fail to keep people informed? Do you lose your temper easily? Do you tend to jump to conclusions before the other person has finished speaking? Do you tend to speak too much and listen too little? Do you sometimes, as an experienced person, forget what it's like to be an inexperienced person? How do you react to mistakes from other people?... are you truly tolerant and helpful in preventing further mistakes by using open-communication, or does the message you communicate make the other person fearful and unwilling to communicate openly? Do you admit <u>your</u> mistakes? One really bad habit is making general assumptions...young men with pony-tail hairstyles don't like hard work. People who don't look you in the eye can't be trusted. Fat people are lazy.

Another really bad habit is being overly critical and even getting some glee out of finding fault with people. If you want to be critical it's a good exercise to listen critically to yourself and to run over the day's interactions critically in your mind. Ask yourself, what would you have done differently if your interest were not self-interest but an honest-to-goodness attempt to give as much as you possibly could to increase understanding? Ask yourself what habits, or fears you have, that should be broken down in the interests of free and open communication. How should you be reacting <u>differently</u>? Where have you become a stick-in-the-mud? How can you hit the ball in a different way to make a better shot down the fairway of open two-way communication?

4.Understand the other person's comfort zones.

The fourth foundation of free and open communication is to understand the other person's comfort zones...and stretch yourself beyond yours.

Everybody has an idea of what they like and what they don't like. What pleases them and what annoys them, or frightens them. They also have an idea of where their capabilities lie and the extent of what they can and can't do. They have a self-image and an ego to satisfy. Some people like to touch the person they're talking to and be touched in response.

Some people freeze up when you touch them. Have you ever advanced physically to speak to someone and they take a step back and fold their arms across their chest? That's because you've entered the "comfort zone" of their body space. They don't feel comfortable with you inside the bubble of space that they're created as a comfort zone around their body.

The stepping back reinstates their border and the folding of the arms across the chest is a symbolic gesture in body language to protect themselves from further intrusion. As conversation progresses and communication begins to be successful the arms will likely come down and the person may even begin to lean forward and shorten the body space between you both, indicating friendly acceptance of you and what you're saying.

The point is that people have comfort zones for each of their beliefs and as a leader in open communication you won't push yourself uninvited into these zones. If, for example, a person is comfortable talking about basic agricultural techniques but you see that they are <u>not</u> comfortable talking about the facts and figures of scientific research that you've come to discuss... then pull back a little before they put up mental barriers against you. Then talk around the zone where they feel comfortable until you feel that they are dropping defences and allowing you in.

The leader will always respect the other person's comfort zones...which might also be personal beliefs. He, or she, will create a climate that is "safe" for the other person. The leader aligns his, or her, style with that of the other person. You notice and respect the safe distance where the other person feels comfortable standing...you assume a relaxed posture with those who might seem tense.

Also, you should use <u>your time</u> the way you assume the other person uses theirs. If they seem a direct and quickly to the point sort of person, you behave in the same way. If the other person tends to spend more time in amiably getting around to the point, you do the same whilst trying to keep the conversation focused. This "echoing", or "mirroring", of the other person's postures and preferred communication style relaxes the other person and helps them to open up. Look around you for examples. Where you see two people locked earnestly and interestedly in conversation they're usually both standing in much the same position. Arms will be in the same position for both people. They will be talking in the same voice tones with much the same expression on each of their faces. This is the situation that you, as a leader, will deliberately set out to create. You do this by learning to have flexible comfort zones yourself...by stretching yourself out of what might make you feel most comfortable in time, space and emotion and aligning yourself with the comfort zones of the other person. This doesn't mean giving up on who you really are...it means having a good understanding of your personal comfort zones and reaching beyond them in the interests of stimulating open communication so as to reach complete understanding

5. Separate the Message from the Messenger!

The fifth foundation for free and open-communication is the ability to separate the message from the messenger. Back in ancient Rome a messenger might have run for a hundred miles bearing a message for Caesar and if Caesar wasn't happy with the message he would have petulantly impaled the messenger. Which is why, in those days, people didn't exactly queue up to be the bearer of bad tidings.

Well, we don't physically kill the messenger anymore but often knowingly, or without our being aware, we do our messengers emotional harm by the way in which we communicate with them.

In salesmanship we're told that first impressions are made in the first six seconds of meeting. Imagine you have someone before you and you've quickly formed the impression that you don't particularly like the person. You don't like the way they look, or the way they dress, the way they sit, or the way in which they speak.

You probably don't like these things because they're not like you! You feel a rising resentment and you become critical, maybe even angry. What is really happening here? You are closing open communication from your end by transmitting hostile emotional messages. And your communication style causes the other person to become fearful, angry, or aggressive, with a result that they too close down on the communication. It isn't necessary for you to like the other person, or even respect their point of view. But you must respect their right to have a point of view and you must remain focused on the message that is being delivered and not the method of delivery, or the person, or personality delivering it.

6. Giving and receiving feedback

The feedback "loop" is a vital part of communication. It's the part of the communication that reinforces that the message has been accurately received. It is also used, positively, to reward and reassure people that what they are doing and what they are feeling is O.K. Also it is used "negatively" when unacceptable behaviour occurs and some "corrective" feedback is called for from the leader. It's essential for leaders to become comfortable with both giving and receiving feedback.

Let's first examine the situation of the leader giving positive feedback.

"Well done Peter..we're all very pleased with the job you did for us. Keep up the good work!"

There you have an example of positive feedback where the speaker hoped to make the other person feel good. It congratulates Peter on his achievement...but Peter still doesn't feel good. What went wrong? The speaker was not <u>specific</u> in his feedback! Peter felt that he was getting a dose of management syrup from someone who was not <u>really</u> aware of the effort that he'd put in. More positive feedback might have sounded like this...

"Peter, I think I speak for all of the team when I tell you how impressed we all were with your report. It must have taken long hours of hard work. We were particularly impressed with your detail on how smaller, faster vehicles could effectively reduce delivery time by sixty per cent. We'll be going over your report carefully...

and we certainly look forward to your next recommendation!"

Giving positive feedback completes the communication circle...the message has been received positively. The leader is happy with the result and the other person feels that his, or her, behaviour has been recognised and rewarded. Now listen to this example of an attempt at positive feedback...can you spot what the speaker did wrong?

*"James I'm really pleased with the report that you turned in last week. The detail on new fabric imports was very impressive and we'll be following up on your suggestions...but while you're here I want to talk to you about some criticisms coming through about your department from production...
...probably one of those interdepartmental jealousies because you're selling out faster than they can make stock. This is what <u>they</u> have to say..."*

What's wrong here is that the speaker is delivering <u>two</u> conflicting messages at the same time. First they are praising the other person by giving positive feedback but before the warm rosy glow can spread she is preparing to deliver negative or corrective feedback. She is using the positive feedback to soften the blow of the bad things to come rather than as a reward for the achievements made... really just making it easier for herself to begin her criticism. The result of this is that the negative cancels out the positive and the message at the receiving end comes out...

You do something right...you do something wrong...you really don't amount to much... do you?

The speaker was also prepared to be indirect and beat around the bush whilst introducing the negative feedback-

"...probably one of those interdepartmental jealousies because you're selling out faster than they can make stock.
This is what <u>they</u> have to say..."

Feedback should always be specific and direct and either positive, or negative but not both at the same time. The speaker had not clearly sorted out what it was that she wanted from the communication. Was the purpose to reward the other person, or to use negative feedback to correct the other person's behaviour? If there were behaviour to be corrected she should have come straight to the point and not have implied that the complaint was nothing to do with her but rather came from the "un-named" individuals over in production. By doing that she was trying to get on the other person's good side before sticking her knife into him.

People generally respond very well to positive feedback, so giving it is your opportunity to open up communication channels, to earn respect and recognition of your authority and to prime your team with motivation. So always be on the lookout for opportunities to give positive feedback where it's due, rather than grasping opportunities to pounce and be critical. In other words, try to catch somebody doing something right!

But sometimes you do have to be critical. When a person's behaviour is causing you a problem you must use negative feedback. But the negative feedback must be used only as a way of correcting the behaviour so as to solve the problem. It must not be used in a personal assault on the other person. In other words, let's fix the problem, not the blame. If you're going to be critical, keep focused on the behaviour. Discuss the behaviour openly and tell the other person how it is affecting you personally. Use "I" messages rather than "you" messages, which are taken as personal and accusative. For example...

"John, I've noticed that you and I are not getting together to discuss your budgetary proposals on a regular basis as was agreed. This is giving me

a real problem because I can't formulate strategy without your figures. Can we talk about that?"

Most managers really don't like to give negative, or corrective, feedback because they feel they won't be liked as a result of it, or that it's an unpleasant task. Then they save up a whole lot of blame and finally dump it all out at once on the poor unsuspecting other party. Don't hold back or save up negative feedback. Leaders realize that they can gain more respect and acceptance by consistently giving constructive corrective feedback...and they choose an appropriate time and place to do it as soon as possible after the problem has shown itself.

You, as a leader, should also look to <u>receive</u> as well as give feedback on your actions and your problem solving. This can also be positive, or negative. In fact you should openly ask for feedback on your ideas and suggestions.

Sometimes by asking someone "Do you have a problem with this suggestion?" or "How do you feel about what I've said?" or simply "Do you have any questions?", you will be breaking tension and getting that person to let out a bottled-up emotion that they were not daring to share with you. If they produce a problem keep focused on the problem - again, don't shoot the messenger -invite them to share their views with you on how the problem might be solved. Let them tell you openly what they want out of it...listen carefully and see how much of what they want you can actually give them.

Thank the person for their feedback and encourage them to follow up with you later on the same issue, so you can discuss progress.

7. Active Listening

The seventh foundation of free and open-communication is <u>Active Listening</u>. Listening is more important than any other communication activity because a study shows that we spend 53% of our time listening and only 16% speaking. Further studies have shown that most of us listen with only 25% effectiveness. Active listening means using all of the senses to focus on the message, so as to obtain maximum understanding. Active listening requires concentration and perception of what lies between the lines. It requires an open mind of the leader and an acute sensitivity to body language.

8. The asking of questions

Asking questions encourages the other person to open up and talk more freely. It helps to develop points further. It provides feedback. It helps the leader to control the communication, bringing it back on track where necessary. It helps the leader to peel off layers surrounding a problem so as to reveal the real issue. Can I have your agreement on this? How did you feel about that? What happened next? What is <u>your</u> perception of the problem? Do you have a solution in mind? All simple questions which, when followed by Active Listening, can be very revealing.

SUMMARY OF EIGHT FOUNDATIONS

Let's summarise the eight foundations of effective open-communication. The first is *looking for good intentions in a relationship rather than a quick fix to the problem*. Leaders are people oriented and use every opportunity to build bridges with people. Leaders are consistent in their attempt to keep open-communication and therefore good and clear understanding as an ongoing, thing with all people involved.

The second foundation we discussed was *Using Authority but not Authoritarianism.* Leaders don't club people over the head with their power, their authority comes to them out of respect earned by their positive actions, particularly by the way in which they communicate.

The third foundation is *Learning to break old Habits.* Leaders first learn to understand themselves so that they can be more flexible and understanding of others.

The fourth foundation for free and open communication is *Understanding other people's Comfort Zones*...and your own. The leader aligns himself with the other person's comfort zone, reflecting the voice tones, speech patterns and body language of the other person.

The fifth foundation is *Separating the Message from the Messenger.* That is, not allowing your judgment, or opinion, to be moved by the personality or physical appearance of the speaker, nor by the way in which they deliver the message.

The sixth foundation is *Giving and receiving feedback.* The leader actively looks for opportunities to give positive feedback. Corrective or negative feedback is also necessary at times and instead of causing dislike and disagreement in the other person, it can be used by the leader to gain more willing compliance and acceptance of the leader's authority.

Active Listening is the seventh foundation. This important skill is used by leaders for 53% of the time taken to communicate.

The eighth foundation for free and open communication is *The Asking of Questions*. Questions followed by Active Listening help fee peel off the layers of the problem to help you get to the heart of the matter. Questions also lead you towards solutions.

SOME USEFUL TECHNIQUES

I now want to introduce you to two useful techniques that leader's use in communication. That is "fogging" and what is called "The Broken Record" technique.

FOGGING
"Fogging" is used when someone is trying to manipulate you into doing or saying something that might suit them, but won't suit you. They might be using too much of your time, or often they will be wanting to dump their problems on you. Or they may be trying to manipulate your emotions with unfair criticism, or provocative statements, so that you become angry and start to lose your

temper. A leader can never get out of control so he uses "fogging". Here's an example...

"It's really difficult to get through all of this work by five o'clock and frankly I think it's time that you and some other managers in this company realized that people like me do have personal lives to get on with after five!"

The leader quickly sees that he can't get drawn into the problem of the speaker having too much work to do. Nor should he respond emotionally to the criticism that he doesn't respect that she has a personal life after five. So he "fogs" the issue by simply responding...

"Yes, I agree that you have quite a bit to do right now..."

...and he then goes on talking about what he wants to communicate. With fogging you find something in the other person's message with which you can agree in principle. You don't fight, or challenge their statements and you don't let them "push your buttons". It's called "fogging" because you can throw whatever you like into a fog and it just disappears. It doesn't reflect, or bounce back at you. If someone continues to challenge you, you just keep agreeing with that part of their statement that you can accept. Or if you can't find anything with which you can agree, at least agree to the possibility that something in their statement is true. Here's another example...

"I don't get nearly enough support for my proposals at the meetings we have. You're the chairman of the committee and so it has to be your fault that sexist decisions are being made!"

Again, the leader doesn't want to get embroiled in the problem at this time and he doesn't want to enter into an argument either. So he uses "fogging"...

"I agree there's a possibility that you're not getting enough support for your proposals... and I am the chairman of the committee".

THE BROKEN RECORD
In management it's always been called The Broken Record technique although today it might be called "The jammed Cd!". The "Broken Record" technique is used when people just don't get your message, or don't want to get your message. For example you might ask a direct question but you don't get a direct answer. In this situation you just try to stay cool and calm and just go on repeating your statement until you do get a direct answer. Here's an example...

Manager
"Did you get the statistics I requested from production and have them typed into the budget document?"

Subordinate
"The budget document is coming along nicely and I expect to have it finished in good time."

Manager
"I'm glad to hear it's coming along well...did you get the statistics from production and incorporate them in the document?"

Subordinate
"I have a million things to do at the moment but I can assure you that the budget document is receiving top priority".

Manager
"I'm also very busy at the moment...<u>did</u> you get the statistics from production and <u>are</u> they typed into the budget document?"

The speaker just goes on like a "broken record" repeating his question, always calmly, always patiently, until he gets a direct answer. The "broken record" technique helps you to stand your ground and to get your message across. Say for example you're busy working on something and someone wants to take up your time..and even dump some of their work on you...here's how you might use the "broken record" technique.

Subordinate to Manager
"Harry, I have a customer coming in, in about half an hour and I need to give him some output figures for one of our new generators...you know all of that stuff better than me, can I talk to you for a moment?"

Manager replies
I'm really sorry Joan I'm very busy I have an important meeting to attend and am preparing for it right now.

Subordinate to Manager
"Harry, this customer spends a lot of money with our company. All I need is a few facts and figures".

The manager then uses the broken record...calmly, patiently repeating exactly the same message.

"I'm sorry Joan, I have an important meeting to attend and I'm busy preparing for it right now".

Dealing with Anger

Let's move on to dealing with using open communication to deal with specific occasions.

First let's consider that the other person is very <u>angry</u>. They storm into your office and explode all over you. You feel your own anger rising and your feeling for self-preservation starts getting into place. What do you do? Well, it would be disastrous for you to lose control. It's very O.K. for you to feel angry because if you entirely bottled up the emotion it would be stressful and the stress would come out in other ways. But you have to control your anger. If the other person is out of control here are the rules for dealing with it.

First get a hold of your own reactions and try to remain calm. Next resist the temptation to interrupt. Let the other person rant on until they've said their piece and the storm has mainly blown over. Don't be tempted to slug it out with them, or to wield your authority at this stage because rage is blind and deaf. At this stage they won't listen to you or see your point of view. If they don't seem to be calming down after a while, interrupt them but only in such a way as to show them that you're listening and that you care about what they're saying. For example..."I can see that you're very angry right now and I hope I'll be able to help you get to the bottom of the problem"......

Then when the initial wave of anger is over proceed as quickly as possible to finding out what the problem is and to working out a solution with the other person. You should talk about the problem and <u>not</u> the person. You should use "I" messages to describe how you feel about the problem and you ask questions to get to the bottom of the problem. Avoid using words like *"You must"..."You should"..."What do you expect after you.."...."It's <u>your</u> fault that..."..."You really ought to..."*. These words tend to promote anger rather than relieve it.

Whilst communicating with an angry person, face them square-on and maintain good eye contact...keep your hands open and palms down and try to keep your body relaxed. Don't fold your arms as this gives the body message that they're not getting through to you. Lean back a little bit so as not to offer an aggressive stance. Keep your face relaxed...don't glare or thrust out your jaw, or get inside the other person's body space.

Once you've heard the problem, if a solution isn't readily available, give assurances that you do take the problem seriously and that you'll get back to them soon with some feedback.

It happens sometimes that there is a volatile and explosive type of person around the office who seems to get angry very often. If this is something that you have to deal with it's probably not the problem they're laying on you that's causing their anger.

They are performing out of their child ego state, stamping and raging, so as to get attention. As fast as you solve their apparent problems they'll come up with new ones because what they really want is attention, reward, recognition and feedback for the job that they do. In this case you should get together with them and offer a job appraisal.

If their work is truly deserving reward make sure that you give them the positive reinforcement that they are seeming to need. If their work isn't up to standard, council them to find out why. Maybe they are getting angry because they don't feel trained well enough to do the job, they don't have the tools or equipment they need, or because some other person, or condition in the workplace is stopping them from achieving the required standards of the job.

Here the important thing to remember is that you can't change people but you can get them to modify their behaviour. So you council people about their behaviour and <u>not</u> about themselves. Listen to the difference in these two statements..

1 *"You seem to take some delight in upsetting everyone in the office. People are complaining about your bad attitude and I have to tell you that in spite of the good results you are achieving you're having a negative effect on morale."*

2 *John, the excellent results you've been achieving lately have obviously been putting you under a lot of pressure and you may not realize it but I feel your communication with the other people in the office seems to be suffering. Could we discuss how that gives me a problem?"*

The first statement is authoritarian. John knows he's in for a dressing down and so his defence barriers go up. The speaker used personal and accusative language to communicate and John now tells her that he feels it's more important to achieve results than pussyfoot around being nice to people who are lesser achievers than he.

John's response to the <u>second</u> statement might have been...
"You're right I <u>have</u> been focused on results but I wasn't aware of upsetting anyone. What's the problem?

There's a world of difference in the two responses.

After describing the actual behaviour, express your feelings and thoughts about the results of the behaviour. What affect is the other person's behaviour having on you personally? How is it giving you a problem? Then specify the <u>behaviour</u> that you want, or prefer. In the example you might specify that you'd like John to treat other people in the office with a little more courtesy. And finally you describe the reward for both of you in him using the suggested behaviour.

To the speaker the reward, which she explains to John, will be in having a good team spirit in the department, which translates into better productivity. It happens sometimes that there is a volatile and explosive type of person around the office who seems to get angry very often. If this is something that you have to deal with it's probably not the problem they're laying on you that's causing their anger.

They are performing out of their child ego state, stamping and raging, so as to get attention. As fast as you solve their apparent problems they'll come up with new ones because what they really want is attention, reward, recognition and feedback for the job that they do. In this case you should get together with them and offer a job appraisal.

If their work is truly deserving reward make sure that you give them the positive reinforcement that they are seeming to need. If their work isn't up to standard, council them to find out why. Maybe they are getting angry because they don't feel trained well enough to do the job, they don't have the tools or equipment they need, or because some other person, or condition in the workplace is stopping them from achieving the required standards of the job.

How do you communicate to someone that their behaviour is unacceptable to you and is causing problems at work? This is a common problem that can promote conflict if not handled correctly. For example, you might have someone working under you who does an excellent job of work in terms of productivity but they upset just about everybody around them along the way. How can open communication help?
To the manager's reward, which is explained to John, will be in having a good team spirit in the department, which translates into better productivity.

Again, in the case of our example, the reward for him will be that those around him will be more helpful and
all of which will help him to maintain, or even exceed, his excellent results..

BEHAVIOUR MODELLING

What we're really talking about here in simple terms is "behaviour modelling". Behavioral scientists tell us that behaviour depends on the reward that comes after it. So if you want to change a person's behaviour you have to ask yourself *what reward are they getting from their present behaviour?* For example an angry person may be seeking the reward of having you take more notice of them. A person who seems to behave negatively all of the time claims for themselves the reward of safety in that they don't have to be responsible for making positive decisions.

If people continue to have their present behaviour rewarded they will not feel a desire to remodel their behaviour. If all I have to do to get your attention is to display anger I'll go right on being angry. If being negative helps me feel safer than being positive I'll go on with a "can't do" rather than "can do" approach to life. To help remodel behaviour you have to offer alternative better rewards for the new behaviour. The angry person might find the reward of being more recognised <u>for their achievements</u> greater than just being noticed in the work place.

The negative thinker might be persuaded that the reward of positive thinking is better prospects, more pay and a brighter future and therefore even greater safety. Behaviour modelling is a big subject.

In simple terms it always requires you to think carefully about the present behaviour and what its rewards are to the person doing it and what behaviour you want, or prefer and what <u>bigger</u> rewards the new behaviour will offer. Here are the four steps again.

1. Describe the actual behaviour without being personal about the one who's doing it.

2. Express your feelings, or thoughts, about the problem that is resulting from the behaviour.

3. Specify the kind of behaviour that you expect, or prefer.
4. Point out to the other person what rewards are to be gained by both of you.
.
RESOLVING CONFLICTS

Let's look now at the subject of <u>resolving conflicts</u> by using open communication. Every leader knows that conflict should be generally avoided...but if conflict is a problem the problem has to be faced. There are times when you just can't agree with the other person...in fact a certain level of conflict is desirable, even necessary, in every progressive organisation. But diversity of opinion can also breed <u>harmful</u> conflict. So how do you manage the conflict?

First try to get all of the facts right and come to your own conclusion about where you really stand. Stick like glue to the facts and don't be influenced by the "messenger". Then decide what role you're going to take in the conflict ahead of you. You have several choices depending on what you want to get out of the conflict. Sharon Crain, a prominent U.S. communications lecturer suggests that you can choose one of five roles.

1. The Steam Roller
2 The Smoother
3 The Side-Stepper
4 The Negotiator
5 The Explorer.

If you feel that there is definitely no room for further discussion you take a tough stand and you "steam-roller" by using your position and your authority. You allow no compromise and you give no concessions. In this role you won't score any points as "Mr Niceguy". Your attitude is *"This is what I want and this is what I expect you to give me".* You might adopt the "steam-roller" position with subversive people...people with whom you've already had a great deal of problems and have unsuccessfully tried other ways of resolving the conflict.

The second position in Sharon Crain's list of roles for dealing with conflict is "The Smoother". Here you give up your position and end up agreeing with the other party because you don't see that there is any other way to end the conflict and you do want to accommodate that person. You don't give up immediately, of course, but after an exchange of views and a token argument "the smoother" decides that he, or she, will ultimately benefit more by changing their position.

The "Side-Stepper" is the next of the five positions to consider. If you know that the circumstances causing the conflict are likely to shift, change, or go-away at some foreseeable time in the future, what is the point of entering into conflict now. Simply "postpone" the conflict until "another time" and just delay going into it.

The fourth and probably the most important position to adopt in conflict resolution is that of "Negotiator". Negotiation is when two or

more parties agree to discuss something with a view to meeting each other somewhere in the middle. In order to do this you must feel that you are prepared to compromise to some extent to find a workable acceptable solution...and you must believe that the other party is also prepared to be flexible. Both parties come out of the negotiation with their self-esteem in tact and their respect for each other still in place. (NB These processes will be described in much greater detail in the second part o this book).
.

The fifth position to consider adopting is that of "Explorer". This position requires parties to work with possible solutions put forward by each of them in order to find the solution that truly satisfies both of them. This is really the best position to be in but it requires acceptance of both parties that they are going to work together in the interests of finding the very best solution.

This can't be done if either, or both parties are angry, unreceptive, or inflexible. To be an "explorer" you need the other person's consent that you both consider it important that a really effective solution is found... and you may need to work on getting this kind of acceptance before you even sit down to problem solving.

Checklist for managing conflict

First choose your fights. Only defend issues which you feel are worth defending - don't get into conflict with someone over a minor issue, or one that doesn't really concern you. Next, do all you can to stop the conflict from getting out of hand. Stay focused on the facts. Define areas of difference including the facts...how you and the other party interpret the facts and the order of their priority. Use plenty of "Active Listening" so you can work out the other person's agenda and maybe even find some sympathy for their viewpoint. Don't hog the conversation - listening will ultimately score you more points than will talking. Paraphrase the arguments that you hear so as to give the other person feedback that you are listening and also so that you can clarify your understanding. Keep the debate focused on common ground, don't let personal alternative agendas creep into the conversation. As talk progresses credit the good points made by the other party so that they don't feel there's a war going on between you. And generally offer suggestions and ideas rather than "laying down the law" and wielding your authority.

I said right at the beginning of this book that "communication" is much more than just "talking". Communication is really a matter of gaining understanding and to do it effectively the leader must first understand himself, or herself and practice mastery of self-control. The leader does not speak to impress but to <u>express</u>.

Because the leader also strives in every way possible to understand the thoughts, feelings, motives and motivations of the other person, he, or she, becomes a student of human nature. Often the most effective communication comes from putting yourself in the shoes of the other person and feeling empathy for their problem. But as a leader you will know that it won't be often that the other person will put themselves into <u>your</u> shoes. They simply won't know how to because they won't have your communication skills.

So as well as understanding you need <u>patience</u> to be an effective communicator ...and you need practice at every available opportunity. You cannot simply listen to a lecture on communication and become a good communicator overnight. Initially you will be able to make some immediate changes to the way you interact with other people. But the valuable change is the gradual process by which you implement what you have learnt on a permanent basis. For this to happen you will pass through four important phases in learning a new skill.

The first stage is where you feel "phoney". The new skill doesn't feel quite right. It isn't you. You feel a little odd and a little out of character using it. But go on using it and it will feel "right"! The second stage is where you feel <u>uncomfortable</u>. At first you won't be ready to deal with the reaction that comes from other people when you start practising the new skill.

You will need to search in your mind for what you have learnt and your own reactions will not be fast, or polished. Particularly, when you are practicing communication skills, it's necessary to think before you speak and you might, at first, feel a little strange when you have to resist replying instantly with the first thought that comes to mind. Don't worry, thinking before you speak <u>will</u> become a reflex action, if you just keep on practising.

The third stage is when you <u>become aware</u> that you are using your new skill. This is when you begin to experience that it works for you, that your new skill pays off. You will be consciously using your new skill and begin enjoying the results that it produces.

And the <u>fourth</u> phase is when using the skill becomes part of your daily behaviour. Every day offers you scores of opportunities to practise the communications skills you've learnt from this programme. Be prepared to go through the "shy" and slightly "uncomfortable" phases one and two in the learning process. Enjoy passing through phase three and recognise your own success in phase four of learning your new skill.

Remember, as a leader, you need to have vision and flexibility and you need to be responsive to change... even if the change that you're faced with, is swopping the old "you" for someone who can <u>really</u> communicate well.

Part TWO
NEGOTIATION

Negotiation is a complex and sensitive issue even at a basic level. It is a skill made up of skills and it is powered by personal motivation.
On the skill-side to become a successful negotiator you will need to practise the skill of creative thinking; the skills of communication, of problem solving, of active listening and even the number one horror of nearly all executives, that of public speaking. You will also need to practise the skill of self-assertiveness. On the motivation side you will need to be of good self-esteem, strongly goal-oriented and anxious to achieve

predetermined results. Clearly "negotiation" is not something that every executive is cut out for...but the <u>leader</u>, the manager who heads a team of "followers", rather than the manager who pushes reluctant people from behind, <u>will</u> need to be able to negotiate and will learn to enjoy negotiation in all its complexity.*

*All of the management skills subjects are available as self-development materials from the publishers Leader's-Edge (RSA) online
www.shop.leadersedge.co.za

In the few pages of this book I will give you vital basics on how to set up a negotiation from the preparation stage through the bargaining stages and on towards reaching an agreement that will satisfy you and your team.

It's true that you won't find the word "negotiation" in the index of many old business text books! But today it's a main word in management because in the higher levels of business <u>nothing</u> gets done without negotiation. I mean by this that almost every transaction and personal interaction that takes place is a kind of "buy and sell" agreement. If you wanted to sell an atomic reactor, negotiation would need to take place.

At the other end of the scale if you wanted to get your assistant to give up his or her precious Saturday morning and come into the office you'd first have to sell them on the idea because in this democratic working world we don't just demand that people do things. That would be demotivational. Leaders can't afford demotivated staff because leadership requires enthusiastic and motivated followers.

So the process by which they'd agree to do it, which is really a matter of your assistant <u>buying</u> your idea that they should come into the office on their day off, would be the process of negotiation. That process might include a "trade-off" in some material terms, like a couple of theatre tickets for Saturday night, or an emotional trade-off of the kind where the one person feels good about helping out the other.

Negotiation literally means *conferring with someone with a view to reaching agreement.*

Any parent will know the process. Negotiation with children takes place continuously. When you promise to read your child a bedtime story if he bathes and gets quickly into bed, you are "conferring with a view to reaching agreement". That is, you are *negotiating*. Back at the office you may be trying to reach agreement over a service contract, some advertising, fleet rental or computer peripherals. Or you may be "conferring with the boss with a view to reaching agreement" on him giving you a raise.

When you think about it your day is filled with negotiations that you take in your stride but you don't <u>call</u> them negotiations. These are just things that you do in your day. Then along comes the big deal, the meeting of the month that is actually called "a negotiation" - you are going to call in the other party, and perhaps their team, and you are going to face them down across the table.

Now why is this so different? Why do most executives fear having to do it? For three reasons.

1.They fear getting into the arena with an opponent who might be stronger than them.

2.They fear losing face and exposure of their weakness by coming off second best in the confrontation.

3. Thirdly most executives are not experienced in drawing together the skills of creative thinking, decision-making, personal intercommunication, salesmanship, active listening and eloquent speaking.

In the final analysis your performance as a negotiator comes down to two factors. Your skills on the one hand - that's your training, experience and know-how - and your motivation on the other - that's your drive, effort, confidence and will to succeed. In other words, you <u>will</u> ...characteristics of a successful negotiator?

A good negotiator must possess a tough aggressive leadership style. Must be dominant and unyielding. Must remain unwaveringly focused on the one key issue. Must win at all costs...must wield heavy authority and take the offensive role. Must always lead first in the negotiation and be seen to do most of the talking. Won't budge from the point in issue unless the other party makes a concession. Sees all negotiation as conflict and a battle to be won....

If you agree with this assessment and feel that's the route to follow you are absolutely...<u>wrong!</u> Today's top negotiators are disciplined without being aggressive, they are creative thinkers who can move flexibly from point to point and back again, if necessary.

 They explore issues which might be outside of the focal issue. They expect to win, yes, but they help the other party also to win. They use integrity rather than authority... and they <u>don't</u> do all of the talking because they know you can often learn more by actively <u>listening</u> to the other party.

Top negotiators are calm, assertive people with a "reasonable" approach to and respect for their opponents. Think of them as good chess players. . They play to win the game, not to beat their opponent into the ground.

What can be negotiated?
Answer..everything! Top negotiators believe that there is nothing that can't be negotiated. If you want a better price on a packet of pencils you can negotiate the price. There is no price on any product in any store or in any warehouse that cannot be negotiated.

There is also no issue of quality, supply, service, terms of delivery, formula, design, format or system that cannot be negotiated. Literally everything is negotiable. Now this doesn't mean that you will always get your own way, that the agreement will always favour you. But you <u>can</u> always *confer <u>with a view</u> to reaching agreeme*nt on anything.

Whether you win or not depends on what is being negotiated and your skill and motivation as a negotiator. And if you do care to take the view that <u>anything</u> can be negotiated, imagine the advantage of scoring a little extra on every deal that you do. And, as you'll learn in from this book you <u>can</u> score extra without necessarily upsetting, or alienating anyone!

Who wins the negotiation?

Negotiations take on many styles requiring many different approaches but there are really only two <u>types</u> of negotiation. The first type is the type where somebody wins the negotiation and somebody loses. This type of negotiation is characterised by one party breaking down the other party so as to gain the major concession. The bargaining is fast. Emotions often become overheated. The stronger negotiator usually wins and an "I win-you lose" situation is created.

This is called a conflict negotiation. Sometimes it might be necessary but conflict bargaining has a serious drawback. That is, the loser will definitely not feel good about losing and will feel <u>bad</u> about ever doing business with you again. If you don't see that you'll ever need to do business again with that person, or that business, all well and good, you might opt for a type-1 negotiation. But in most business dealings we would hope for a residual pool of goodwill after the bargaining is done and the agreement is signed.

This is because we hope to go on doing business with the other party...and because

they are an important part of the environment in which we do business and their endorsement of us as reasonable and fair people is important.
Where an ongoing business relationship must be built, negotiation takes the form of a creative shifting towards agreement. Deliberate, planned, negotiation takes place step by step. Both parties try to avoid conflict and rather "collaborate" towards an agreement where both parties win.

All very well, you may say, but what happens if you go in using the collaborative type - 2 negotiation approach and the other party comes blazing in with a "winner-take-all" or conflict-bargaining approach? You deal with it through carefully? preparation during the five stages of a negotiation. Let's have a look at the five stages one by one.

THE FIVE STAGES OF A NEGOTIATION

As we said earlier, without perhaps realising it, you already spend a large part of your day in negotiation. In fact wherever and whenever you are involved in a situation where you need to shift someone towards agreement with you, you are in fact negotiating. The following five stages will be useful to remember for any type of negotiation but let's consider that we have a substantive issue before us. Two stages must take place <u>before</u> the negotiation and three stages during the negotiation.

Stage 1 - Research
The first stage before the negotiation is <u>research</u>. If it's a big important negotiation the amount of research you do will be proportionate to your success in winning the negotiation. You need full background on the issue to be negotiated <u>and</u> on the people on the other side...your opponents in the negotiation. What statistics are going to be important? What can you find out about quality, price, industry standards and controls, competitive activities in the market place? What about deliveries? What quantities will be at issue and what will be the timing required?

Are there time restraints that might favour you, or the other party? What are the required specifications? Is there any flexibility on the specifications?   What material and human resources will be required and what are the logistics of meeting the demand?

Make sure you are truly aware of what the issue to be negotiated really is, from your point of view, and thoroughly investigate <u>everything</u> that's likely to come up in debate surrounding that issue.
Then investigate everything that might be to your advantage to know about the other party.

Know your strengths and weaknesses... also investigate the probable strengths and weaknesses of your opponents. It might help you to know that they are over-geared and might have a poor cash flow...that they are involved in a diversification programme and what they need from you is vital for their new operation.

Or that they are expanding and are acquiring new equipment and machinery. Is there anything that you can do, or stop doing, that will strengthen your position and weaken theirs? Are they a top negotiating team used to getting their own way, if so what can you find out about their tactics? Will it be a single person, or a team? Will the team be mostly managerial, or mostly technical? Who is the main decision-maker? What do you know about him and his negotiating style? The more sound research you have the better your chances of success at the negotiating table. And top negotiators do this well in advance and not on the way to the Other Party's office on the day of the negotiation.

Stage 2 - Planning
The second of the two pre-negotiation activities is PLANNING. In this activity you plan how you want the agreement to take place. How you will attempt to steer the

negotiation in the direction of an acceptable outcome for you?

The first thing to plan is, what issues are to be negotiated. Let's say the subject to be negotiated is the sale of a warehouse. Whether it should be sold, or not is not up for debate, both parties have agreed on this. The main issue might be price. That's what the negotiation is going to be about on the face of it. But the creative thinker would work out that other issues could influence the negotiation, such as terms of payment, such as fully repaired or "as is", such as favoured date of transfer.

A top negotiator would select four major issues...in this case price, terms of payment, fully repaired or not, and transfer date. These would be entered on a planning sheet as key words to be used in the negotiation.
The next stage in the planning activity is to know what outcome you will be hoping for from each of the four issues. Plan what is the very best possible outcome that you could hope for. On our planning sheet we'll call that "Most acceptable". Next, what would be an <u>acceptable</u> outcome... not the greatest that you could hope for but nonetheless a pretty good acceptable deal? Third, what would be the <u>least acceptable</u> outcome...one that won't

make you delirious with joy but one that you'll accept only if you have to?

So we have three headings:
"Most Acceptable", *"Acceptable"* and *"Least Acceptable"*.

Now if you take your planning sheet and write the four issues down the left side...in this case "Price", "Terms", "Repaired" and "Transfer Date". Across the top of your planning sheet write "Most Acceptable", "Acceptable" and "Least Acceptable" and draw three columns down the paper. So you have the four headings for the issues on the left and the three degrees of acceptability along the top.

What you have here is no less than eighty-one permutations of the deal that you can negotiate! That's <u>creative</u> planning! Imagine, you are armed with a planning sheet like this and the other guy comes in focused only on the one issue of price linked to the highest reward he, or she can think of. Who is likely to be the most flexible and creative negotiator? Who is likely to win the negotiation? You are!

But the planning activity does not stop at the issues to be negotiated, or the possible outcomes that <u>you</u> foresee.
Now you need to put yourself into the other party's shoes and do some creative thinking.

What issues are they likely going to debate and what outcomes are _they_ likely to want from the negotiation? Consider that the other party's need will be quite different to your own need...what is their _greatest_ need? What would you consider to be their highest expectation from the negotiation? What are _they_ likely to consider a good deal?

What is the least they're likely to accept...and very important indeed, what will happen in your camp, or theirs, if the negotiation deadlocks? How will their timing be affected...will they, or you, have something to gain by stalemating the negotiation, or even walking out on it? If you only think about what outcomes _you_ want, you won't be able to bargain and you'll definitely lose the negotiation because the negotiator on the other side is likely to be doing _his_ homework on you!

Questions to ask yourself at the planning activity... what type of negotiation is this likely to be? Conflict Bargaining, where winner takes all and you won't necessarily part friends, or Mutual Interest bargaining, where both parties shift towards agreement with the idea of both winning something and remaining on a good business footing with each other?

Or will there be a tendency for the negotiation to deteriorate from mutual-interest bargaining to conflict-bargaining?

Is it likely that the negotiation can be settled at one sitting? Or will it be an on-going negotiation? Are the Unions involved? Have they been invited? Where will the negotiation take place? Does this venue give you, or the other party any strategic advantage? <u>When</u> will the negotiation take place? Are you being rushed into it by the other party so giving them an advantage, or are you taking advantage of timing? What will the seating arrangement be at the venue? Can it be arranged to your advantage?

You don't have to be as obvious as sitting their team on two-foot high wooden stools whilst your team towers over them in four- foot leather-bound executive swivel chairs but tactical advantages can be scored through seating arrangements which immediately set the climate for the negotiation: hostile conflict bargaining or collaborative, mutual-respect bargaining. Whilst thinking about the venue set-up, will you need overhead projection, or audio-visual equipment, microphones, a flip chart, board and chalk? Now is the time to plan these things..to check that you have them, that they work properly <u>and</u> that you know how to operate them efficiently.

And don't rely on using the other party's equipment. It may just be that the projector works perfectly for their presentation but for some unaccountable reason the fuse blows when it's your turn!

Also as part of the pre-negotiation procedure ask yourself these questions regarding your case and the other party's case. In your opponent's case....are you ready to question <u>their</u> facts and figures; their assumptions and their conclusions? Are you ready to fill in what they may have unintentionally, or purposefully omitted? Are you ready to amplify any weakness and use it to consolidate your own position? Will you allow your opponent to go first in the negotiation, or will you attempt to lead? Can you gain advantage by having the other party lead, in that you can first find out what their demands are, before you present your case? Or would it be to your advantage to lead first so as to set your own tone for the negotiation... either mutual-agreement, or conflict-bargaining? What do you know about the tactics of the other party and how should you prepare to meet these tactics?

Also, what do you know about the <u>personality</u> of the other party... do they easily become overheated and emotional, are they a "must win everything on the table" personality that favours conflict bargaining? How experienced will they be at negotiating? And very important, does the other party have the <u>authority</u> to reach agreement with you...to actually sign the agreement? If the top person at the other side must report back for higher authority, you may not wish to negotiate with them in the first place.

In consideration of your own case... what method will you use to best demonstrate, show, or prove the benefits of your case to the other party? How will you maximize the strength of your own case whilst maximising the <u>weakness</u> of theirs? How will you protect your weaknesses from being exploited and maximised by the other party? Do you know the facts and figures of your case inside and out so that you're ready to answer any question, or suggestion, to your advantage?

GIVING AND TAKING CONCESSIONS

The reason for the negotiation is to confer with a view to reaching agreement. This means that each player at the table will attempt to creatively shift the other party towards agreement by means of giving and taking "concessions". The party that gains more for giving less gets the best of the bargain.

Now you have already planned the "Most Acceptable", "Acceptable", and "Least Acceptable" outcomes that you want from the situation. Better still for each of <u>four</u> possible situations (such as Price, Terms, Transfer Date, and Repairs as in the sale of a warehouse example we gave you earlier). Now it isn't likely that you will achieve <u>any</u> of the hoped-for outcomes without having to give something away to the other party.

So you have to plan in advance what concessions you might be prepared to give in return for what advantage gained from the other party. Think of it as a pack of cards of different values ranging from high to low. Nobody must know what's on the face of the cards except you, or your team. You can't know, for sure, prior to the negotiation what concession cards the other player will have in his hand, or up his sleeve, but you can imagine what the other party can afford to give from the research you did earlier... and you can also imagine how tough it's going to be to get concessions out of the other party from your research into what kind of player he, or she is!

SUMMARY OF THE PRE-NEGOTIATION

Everything that's been said so far concerns pre-negotiation. Let's summarize before we go to the presentation table and begin to bargain. First understand what a negotiation is...a negotiation is conferring with another party with a view to reaching agreement. And there are basically two types of negotiation. That is the I win-you lose type which is likely to take the form of conflict bargaining.

There's also the type of negotiation where both parties arrive at a mutual agreement where, in the end, they're both happy with the outcome. If you want to go on doing business with the other party the second type of bargaining, where everybody wins something, is preferable. If you don't intend to work with the other party again, or see no advantage to building a long-term relationship, if the point in question demands aggressive negotiation of a fast and emotionally charged nature, then conflict-bargaining, or the "fight path" may be the route to take.

But generally it's not good to consider that a negotiation is a battlefield where you're out to annihilate the other party. Generally a good negotiator aims to leave the table leaving the other party satisfied with the deal and the way in which the deal was reached.

Approach negotiation in a spirit of fairness and co-operation. Use <u>integrity</u> to overcome emotional barriers and <u>creativity</u> to get over stumbling blocks, or deadlocks. Negotiation should not become a battle of wills, where one side takes the stand that they are 100% right and the other side is definitely wrong!

The process begins with <u>research</u> and <u>planning</u> and it's best not to do this on the way to the airport!
Get all of the facts and figures that you need to support your argument. Know in advance exactly what it is that you want to negotiate. Plan four strategic situations likely to have a major bearing on the negotiation.....
On a planning sheet write down the "most acceptable", the "acceptable" and the "least acceptable" outcomes for each of the four situations.

Learn as much as you can about your opponent. What is their background? What are <u>their</u> facts and figures? What is the most they will expect...what is the least they'll likely settle on? What is their negotiating style? What are their strengths and weaknesses...how will you minimise their strengths and maximise their weaknesses? And how will you maximise your strengths and protect your weaknesses?

From your research and planning you will have a good idea how to proceed even if it's going to be a quick and heated round of conflict bargaining... but before you go to the bargaining table have an idea what kind of concessions will be available from you in return for what kind of concessions might be available from the other party. Then be prepared to give <u>nothing</u> away that doesn't take you a step forward.

One more thing before you go into the negotiating forum. It's vital that you prepare your self for "Active Listening". If you are going to spend half of your time "listening" don't sit there passively listening. That is with your ears open but your mind closed....or focused solely on what <u>you</u> are going to say next. Active listening is interpreting the other party's real needs by not just accepting what they <u>say</u> they need but by reading the signals surrounding their speaking.

What do they <u>really</u> want from the negotiation? You must also focus your attention and strain for facts and figures that will help your case, build your arguments, or produce evidence that you can use. Think what may have been left out of the other party's presentation and why. Listen for signs of the other party's emotional state..and look for signs of body language or non-verbal signals that help you form a picture of the other party.

Listen actively by taking notes, making "mind-maps". Fix the speaker with good eye-contact. Lean forward from time to time and give nods of assent. Paraphrase certain of the speaker's points so as to make sure you've understood his message.

A good negotiator knows that listening can often get him further than speaking, so he moves his mouth before his brain has gone into gear. At all times during the negotiation he, or she, maintains a balance between active intelligent listening and effective speaking.

THE NEXT STEP

The research and pre-negotiation has taken place and now is the time to meet the other party face-to-face and to get the negotiation opened. Top negotiators tend to be "cool" people who don't get emotionally overheated and who *never ever* charge like a bull at the gate. There is a procedure to follow and distinct moves to be made.

- **Stage 3 – The presentation**

The climate has been set by choice of venue...the other party's place...your place, or a mutually agreed terrain. Both parties meet and the skilful negotiator begins immediately to break the ice. Tension is high because no-one wants to lose on the deal, or lose face in the negotiation.

Each party will be weighing each other up. An unskilled negotiator might plunge in with his bid, or a demand, or a probing and hostile question such as "have you destroyed many historic buildings this year in your recreation plan?" after only a perfunctory handshake. But a skilled negotiator will spend several minutes clearing away as much tension as possible by <u>not</u> talking about the deal to be made, or the dispute to be settled. His, or her background research will have told something of the other party that might make useful light conversation...some reference to sport, a new activity of the company not related to the negotiation, the area where the other person lives, polite chat, perhaps, about the journey to the venue.

The other party must be put at ease and right from the start both parties should aim at a spirit of co-operation..
If you do get the "bull charging head on" in the first minute of the meeting, you do what a bull fighter does. You side-step the issue and

politely say..."If you like we can put that on the agenda when we're seated and we can address your concerns"... and move onto another subject of less intensity. Where a team of people from each side enter a room, a good negotiator will immediately attempt to keep them standing and to split them into groups of two, or three people who would be at the same level on the opposite team.
Getting them talking off the record on simple unrelated matters, before getting seated, is far better than having them glare aggressively at each other across a boardroom table.

The ice is broken..
Everyone is seated and time now becomes precious. At this stage the focus comes under four headings. They are:

1 The Purpose
2 The Plan
3 The Pace
4 The Personalities

Again your research and planning will have given you the background that you need.
The purpose is why you are here. *The matter where agreement must be reached.* For example the old warehouse on the waterfront that is to be bought, or sold.

The plan is the topics surrounding the issue to be discussed and the order in which you will work through them... for example the price ...terms of payment, renovation, or complete site clearance, most favourable transfer date. The plan is really the agenda for the meeting. The third "P" is for pace ...how much time will you allot to each topic...how long do you anticipate for the entire meeting?

The fourth "P" is for personalities ...who is finally at the meeting, what are their contributions likely to be? .
At this point you should determine whether one, or more of the personalities has the authority to sign off the deal. If not, you will immediately know that the other party are viewing your meeting as a "fact-finding" mission rather than a serious attempt to reach agreement at this time.

These four matters of "Purpose", "Plan", Pace" and "Personalities" are tabled by both parties for agreement. It could be as simple as this. . .

"Ladies and gentlemen..thank you for coming. I believe that you have been informally introduced. We know that your waterfront warehouse is for sale. My company has interest in purchasing it for redevelopment as part of a recreation area and today we'd like to

negotiate an acceptable price with you as well as terms of payment, timing of transfer and the issue of whether you would renovate it, whether we would take it "as-is", or whether we would demolish and rebuild to our specification. We felt that we should be able to cover each of the four main issues on the agenda in twenty minutes and leave a further half hour to see if we can reach final agreement. Can we agree on the agenda and the timing and get the meeting underway? Thank you...fine! If we could now just be introduced formally so that we know to whom we must address specific questions and what their respective contributions are likely to be, we can get underway".

But what happens if there is no general agreement over the purpose, plan and pace that you've proposed? Or even the personalities present? What if the other party simply doesn't agree with the procedure? Well, if you sense that the spirit of co-operation won't be there from the word "go" and you won't be able to shift the other party towards agreement with mutual-interest bargaining, you may have to switch your strategy to one of "conflict-bargaining".

No more "Mr Nice Guy. It's going to be rough and you will need a <u>defensive</u> or <u>offensive</u> strategy. But this is a last resort. Even if you have to start off with a conflict bargaining strategy it would be best if you can steer the negotiation, later, back onto the mutual-interest strategy. Do this by removing the other party's fears and giving reassurances that you have their interest at heart as well as your own. Try to stay calm and keep your head when all others around you are getting steamed up and losing theirs!

If YOU are not happy with the agenda, or the timing, now is the time to request changes after which both parties stick to the agreed timing and procedure.

This first agreement by both parties further reduces tension and hostility and immediately gives a sense of co-operation. Agreement on procedure and plan, allows a mechanism for those who rush down a new and different path to be called back on track. Agreement on "pace" allows the negotiation to be kept inside an agreed time frame.

Now we get down to the real business of the negotiation...the fourth stage   .....
The first two stages we have discussed are the pre-meeting work of <u>research</u> and <u>planning</u>. The third stage is that of <u>presentation</u>. And the fourth stage is "bargaining".

Stage 4 – The Bargaining
A sensitive issue in negotiation is who is going to take the lead? Who will present first? More often the <u>seller</u> will lead before the <u>buyer</u> and the <u>host</u> will lead before the <u>visitor</u> but there is no hard and fast rule. A time, or pace, has been agreed upon by both parties...so the time should be shared equally between the parties, certainly during the opening procedure.

Initially both parties should aim for short exchanges with plenty of questions and answers. Each should offer the other ample opportunity to make comments and, as far as possible, to be supportive of each other's arguments. At this stage of the process active listening is very important and so is plenty of interaction. No one party should, at the opening, go into any lengthy submissions.

Then one party will take the lead by laying down an opening bid on one of the major issues. If you go in to bat first you may have the tactical advantage of setting the scene by being the first major speaker. But you must also consider that the first bid is highly revealing. It immediately shows the other party how you are thinking. If you are selling the waterfront warehouse and you table your price at, say, one point five million, the other party <u>knows</u> that you have tabled your highest expectation, or "most acceptable price". They will be interested in your "least acceptable price" which they will now be able to guess at around the million mark.

Their counter bid will then come in around six hundred thousand leaving room to negotiate up to around seven hundred and fifty or eight hundred thousand. Until they <u>knew</u> your opening bid they may have thought that you'd ask two million and may therefore have been prepared to make an opening bid of nine hundred thousand.

The opening bid must be made firmly and with authority. If you are the seller start off with the highest <u>defensible</u> bid. If you are a buyer, make your lowest <u>defensible</u> offer. You must be able to defend your bid with facts and figures, with reason and logic. If you are just bluffing, or throwing numbers down, the other party will soon know that you are unprepared for the negotiation and they'll be looking forward to winning over you. If you can't justify your bid, don't make it.

Remember these three points

1. The Opening Bid sets parameters and a top, or bottom limit.
2. Your bid influences the Other Party's bid.

3 Your bid must be defensible and still leave enough room for you to manoeuvre and make concessions.

The Opening Bid must be made assertively, firmly and clearly without any amplification. There should be no attempt to justify the price, or any other part of the bid until the other party's bid is received. Although it *is* acceptable to ask for clarification on the bid, so that both parties can be quite sure that they understand the bid correctly.

 If you <u>are</u> asked by the other party, *"How do you arrive at that offer?"* you must side-step the question with a question of your own. *"I'll be happy to explain that to you but can I first know what figure you had in mind - we can then get down to how we arrive at our price and you can explain your bid. Is that O.k. with you?"*

The Opening Bid will usually have more components than just "price". It will also comprise items such as delivery, payment terms, quality, engineering specifications, time constraints..and so on.

As the bargaining continues you must be prepared to be pushed on these issues. In your pre-negotiation work of research and planning you identified the major issues that you thought would be tabled and you took the four major issues. You then worked out a "Most Acceptable", "Acceptable" and "Least Acceptable" outcome for each of the major issues. This gives you three times three, times three, times three, possible outcomes. That's 81 different options.

Each is a possible "card" that you can select to offer as a concession as the bargaining continues. And this is where the <u>creativity</u> of negotiation comes in. The other party may need a concession from you before they can move. So you give away one of your "least acceptable outcome" cards...but in return you attempt to pick up one of their "most acceptable outcome" cards. The other party won't easily go for this but they may table one of <u>their</u> "least acceptable outcome cards".

A concession that you give must at least be matched in equal value by one that they give... and the pace of the concession giving must be at least similar. If you give a little there can be no forward movement until they have given a little in return. Concessions must be creatively traded. You should fully appreciate their value to you and their <u>probable</u> value to the other party. And they should be reserved for the time in the negotiation when you think you're going to need them.

Always remember, what you want is not necessarily what the other party needs. You may be focused on price. They may be focused on quality and delivery.

Again, use creative thinking to help the other party see that the concession you are giving is significant and meaningful. All concessions given should be made at a measured pace towards the projected outcome.

Two more things about concessions... don't let concession-trading form too much of a pattern. Concentrate on the main issue of where the negotiation is leading rather than developing a "one-for-you/ one-for-me" line of thought. And second, don't be afraid to pick one of your concession cards up again and put it back into your pack.

For example
"I can see that price is vital for you but we'd be extremely stretched to meet that price <u>unless</u> we could review our agreement on payment terms".

So the negotiation is underway and you can now feel glad about the research and planning that went in before the negotiation, whether it's the conflict type of negotiation, or the collaborative type of negotiation that you're now into. Your presentation has been made, your opening bid has been tabled and their opening bid has been offered in return...and the bargaining is taking place with concessions being offered by both parties in an attempt to reach agreement.

Be patient. No negotiation is instantly resolved. If you wanted to buy my house and I instantly accepted your first offer you'd definitely be unhappy because you'd think there was something wrong with the house. Or that you'd paid too much for, it!
Both parties move slowly but deliberately towards agreement.
Each side looks not only for concessions that might be agreeably traded but for <u>benefits</u> that can be presented to support their sales argument.
Creative thinking helps see what the other party wants and needs. You must be dedicated to satisfying those wants and needs as far as possible <u>without</u> giving away too much of what you want and need. All very well, you say, but it's not always smooth and easy. . .what if you <u>deadlock</u> and there's no forward movement?

Top negotiators avoid deadlock at all costs by making every attempt to keep the negotiation fluid and moving in a positive direction. But it does happen that both parties dig in and neither will budge, say, on an issue of price.

Now you must examine the real issues. Can the other party really not move further towards you, or are you perhaps dealing with a negotiator who feels he must make a stand to save face?

In other words is it a business issue, or a <u>personal</u> issue? If it's personal, how can you help him to save face., is there another concession you can trade? If "price" is really the dispute can you restart the meeting by talking about change in specification, terms of delivery, or trade-in terms. If all else fails...take a break. Maybe go out, informally, to lunch with the other party so as to change the mood and the climate. Or call for a recess so as to re-examine your research material for possible new support material. Or call for a change of team member so as to bring in a new expert with a fresh perspective. Or call for higher authority...bring in the big boss as a strategic move. Even suggest to them that <u>they</u> call in higher authority!

Incidentally here's a good tip if the negotiation is important. Keep a hot-line open back to some expert opinion in another office, or another building, so that you can instantly reach them by telephone. You might also consider taking a lap-top computer with you for fast access to any data required.

All very well when reasonable people are talking to reasonable people. But how does one handle it when the other party comes out fighting as soon as the first bell is rung? How do you win the fight? The fighter is the tough authoritarian executive who likes to talk down at you from a power base. He, or she, doesn't care for breaking the ice and they launch straight into the attack. They expect to pick up major concessions by slamming you back against the wall, so to speak. And they are often prepared to be personal in their attack to the point of rudeness.

Because they talk from a stronger power base than yours, they are not interested in creating goodwill, or shifting towards agreement. They know that you need them more than they need you..and they're about to let <u>you</u> know it! It's also part of their plan to not only win the negotiation but to beat the other negotiator into the ground!

Stay calm in the face of this unpleasant onslaught. Side-step immediate deep probing questions and do all possible to establish a procedure. In negotiation there's a concept that "he who controls the battleground controls the skirmishes". So try to focus the opening discussion back onto the issue of "purpose", "pace" and "plan".

Don't be drawn into an argument but do remain assertive. Don't let the fighter dominate you, or intimidate you in the opening stages by giving you an inferior seating arrangement... an uncomfortable obscure position with the sun in your eyes, for example. (Especially as this type of person may have already left you alone in reception for twenty minutes before the meeting, just to work on your nerves!).

Keep coming back to the Purpose, the Pace and the Plan. That's the "battleground". The fighter will want to run free. Keep bringing him back to the agreed plan. Don't allow deadlock. Keep things moving but don't bother to look for a creative movement towards agreement. This person is insensitive to all but their own needs. Your trump card is that you have something that they want., it must be so or they wouldn't be speaking to you. So it boils down to a straight compromise. If they want 1000 and you think it's worth only 750, bargain slowly up to your limit.

I say slowly because it will be hard bargaining. The fighter does not want to trade you concession for concession. He, or she expects two concessions from you for every one that they give... they may even expect to pick up all of the concessions and give none. Remain calm and try not to be forced into emotional behaviour. Remain assertive. Keep controlling the battlefield by bringing the fighter back to the agreed procedure.

What if the fighter loses his temper and displays anger and aggression?

This is not acceptable behaviour in any kind of negotiation. You would then need to suspend the negotiation and walk out. If the Other Party really wants what you have, they'll get back to you. Otherwise you're anyway wasting your time. When entering into conflict bargaining it's always an option to "get-up-and go" and this does not mean that you'll lose the negotiation in the end. How many times have you seen politicians "walk-out" over an issue only to be back in their benches, smiles on their faces, the very next day?

Stage 5 – The Agreement
The fifth and final stage in the negotiating process is The Agreement stage. The hard-bargaining is done. Concessions have been exchanged and picked up by both parties. The tension has eased and everyone begins to relax over the formality of tying up the details and finally drafting the agreement.

Beware!! This is a very dangerous time because just as the deal is about to be closed the skilled negotiator will often spring once more to life and try for one last "nibble" at the cake. When a salesman sells you a suit he tries to trade the sale up by also selling you a shirt, a tie and a pair of shoes and socks. This is because he knows that he has your confidence ...that you have reached agreement on the major issue and that you have gone into a buying mode. Your guard is down and you may be vulnerable. If your deal is over computer hardware, for example, be prepared for a request to throw in a service contract, or extra supplies of peripherals or software <u>after</u> all the bargaining has been done and agreement has been reached but <u>before</u> the draft agreement is signed. Even be prepared, if necessary, to re-enter the bargaining phase and patiently go another round over the newly introduced issues.

SOME TACTICS THEY MAY TRY ON YOU!

During the negotiation "tactics" may be used on you by seasoned negotiators. Here are some of the old classics to look out for and what you do when you meet them.

GOOD GUY/ BAD GUY
You've seen this in the movies. A pair of cops are interrogating a suspect. One acts really mean and tough. The other is gentle and reasonable. Well, they also turn up as a pair of

negotiators. The "bad-guy" will table a very low bid with great assertiveness and authority.

When you wince at this the "good-guy" appears to help by offering a higher bid, probably with more strings attached. The two of them appear to be in disagreement ...the good-guy says he feels he can stick to his end if you hurry and take his bid now... and you are being rushed into making a decision around a bid that is also probably much too low. If you see this tactic being played on you just gently expose it for what it is...say for example "Guys can we drop the act and really get down to the issue?"

THE WALL OF SILENCE
The Wall of Silence is another tactic. If you suddenly find that you are doing all of the talking... and in fact filling in the silences by answering your own questions. Here the Other Side is letting your "motormouth" blabber on whilst they are actively listening for your give-aways. If you feel this is happening to you, ask a question and then treat them to a dose of silence whilst you actively listen. They will soon break the embarrassing silence.

THE FALSE ISSUE

The False Issue is an important weapon in the tactics armory. Here the negotiator focuses on an issue such as delivery, pretending that this is his major concern...meanwhile his major concern is price. He then allows himself to be beaten into giving a major concession on delivery, which doesn't really concern him, whilst he gets the better deal on price. The Other Side has happily taken a major concession, or so they think, whilst the negotiator has won his most important issue with a "most acceptable" outcome. Skillfully used, this one is hard to counter. Your research at the beginning and your probing questions during the bargaining, along with active listening, are likely to expose the bluff.

LACK OF AUTHORITY

Lack of Authority is a frequently used tactic. When the one party is pushed into a corner with a hard-to-refuse request, they simply say that they personally don't have the authority to agree on that issue. This might be true. In which case it's very disruptive to the negotiation. Or it might be a bluff. Right at the beginning of the negotiation when we spoke of the four "P's of Purpose, Plan, Pace and Personalities, it should have been established who had authority for what agreements to be made. If the Other Party pleads lack of authority at an advanced stage, you have to offer every facility to get the required authority. Offer fax and telephone and computer facilities, even an overnight stay if necessary. Or call for higher authority to be made present in person. The same goes for when the negotiation is made to falter by a comment like...."I can't agree to something like that without consulting my production manager". Then you try to bring in the "expert"; by fax, email, SMS, phone, or in person, without allowing the negotiation to recess.

TIME CONSTRAINTS
Time Constraints is another tactic in frequent use and this is a nasty attempt to pressurize you at the last minute into accepting your "least acceptable" outcome.

Maybe the Other Side knows that you have a plane to catch. They know that you'll lose face if you go home without the deal. They also know from the preliminary opening agreement what pace was agreed upon for the negotiation. You are almost out of time and they have dragged the negotiation out avoiding agreement on the major issues.

They feel that you'll take a bad deal for yourself rather than no deal at all..so they save all of the real negotiation for you at the airport lounge, where they've kindly offered to lift you. At this point it's up to you to know whether to take the "least acceptable" outcome, to reschedule for a further round, or to scrap the negotiation. If you can pick up on the tactic earlier... get them back on track by reminding them of the procedure, or why you are here and what the negotiation is about, and the pace that was agreed to deal with each issue.

Beware right at the preliminary ice-breaking session when the personalities are meeting you out of town and someone asks you the innocent question...when are you going back?

TAKE A BREAK
Let's take a break is a tactic to use when hard bargaining is moving towards deadlock. Completely change the venue...go up to the golf club and have coffee, or lunch. Recess and try to introduce some informality into the meeting. This tactic can be useful for both parties.

THE WALK-OUT
The Walkout is the most disruptive and demonstrative action, or tactic, a negotiator can make. If a party can't reach agreement on even its least acceptable planned outcome, a walkout becomes likely.

If a negotiator is faced with aggressive, or violent behaviour he will suspend and walk out. But a walkout can be just a tactic. If the one party has a strong power base and knows that you are really keen to reach agreement, they may stage a walkout as a token of their strength, leaving you talking to the ceiling. Then, when tempers have cooled, comes round two of the negotiation.

You are now going to be aware of the other party's strength and will be expected to quiver in anticipation of them acting demonstrably again, if you don't give them their own way! Because a walkout is highly disruptive and may also be very expensive it's a tactic to be avoided. Patient, flexible and assertive negotiation that sticks to The Purpose, The Plan, The Pace, and as far as possible, the original Personalities, is the way to go.

SUMMARY
This part of the book describes in full measure the process of negotiation as usually applied to a quite sizeable sit-down deal. You have been introduced to the FIVE basic stages of negotiation which are:

1. Research
2. Planning
3. Presentation
4. Bargaining

5. Agreement

As discussed earlier, just about everything is negotiable and daily you will be faced with a need to create winning situations that require agreement from another party – even if you need your teenage son to "buy" your idea of him washing and polishing your car.

You may not need to spend much time on planning and research if the negotiation is a small matter. But even in small matters the principles of *presentation, bargaining and reaching agreement* should readily spring to your mind. Negotiation is most definitely a skill and like all skills it should be practiced at every opportunity where you would hope to gain an advantage.

FURTHER STUDY

Negotiation is a complexity of skills and ability driven by strong motivation and defined, goals...and it is an <u>essential</u> amongst the many developed talents of the true leader in management. Further self-learn management materials covering several important skills subjects (time management, assertiveness training, team-building, memory training, motivation etc) are available online direct from the publishers Leader's-Edge (RSA)

shop.leadersedege.co.za
email: info@leadersedge.co.za

www.ingramcontent.com/pod-product-compliance
Lightning Source LLC
Chambersburg PA
CBHW061515180526
45171CB00001B/194